To Sande

From Brenda

YOU'RE a GOOD human

(THANKS FOR THAT!)

YOU'RE A LOT OF REALLY *GOOD* THINGS (ALL IN) ONE PERSON.

Like how you know
when something's
important and you
give it attention.

OR WHEN *something*
NEEDS A LITTLE

SILL

NESS,

YOU KNOW HOW TO share a LAUGH.

YOU GOT THIS!

WAY TO GO!

You're
someone
who believes
in the best
of others...

BECAUSE you always GIVE THE best of you.

YOU ARE
GENUI

NELY

YOU, ALL OF THE TIME.

(THANKS FOR THAT.)

BEING around YOU IS THANKFULLY NEVER awkward.

In fact,
having you
nearby is one of
the best things
there is.

YOU JUMP (IN WHEN) someone NEEDS HELP, NOT HESITATING ONE BIT.

When something
is lost, you're
the first person
to start looking.

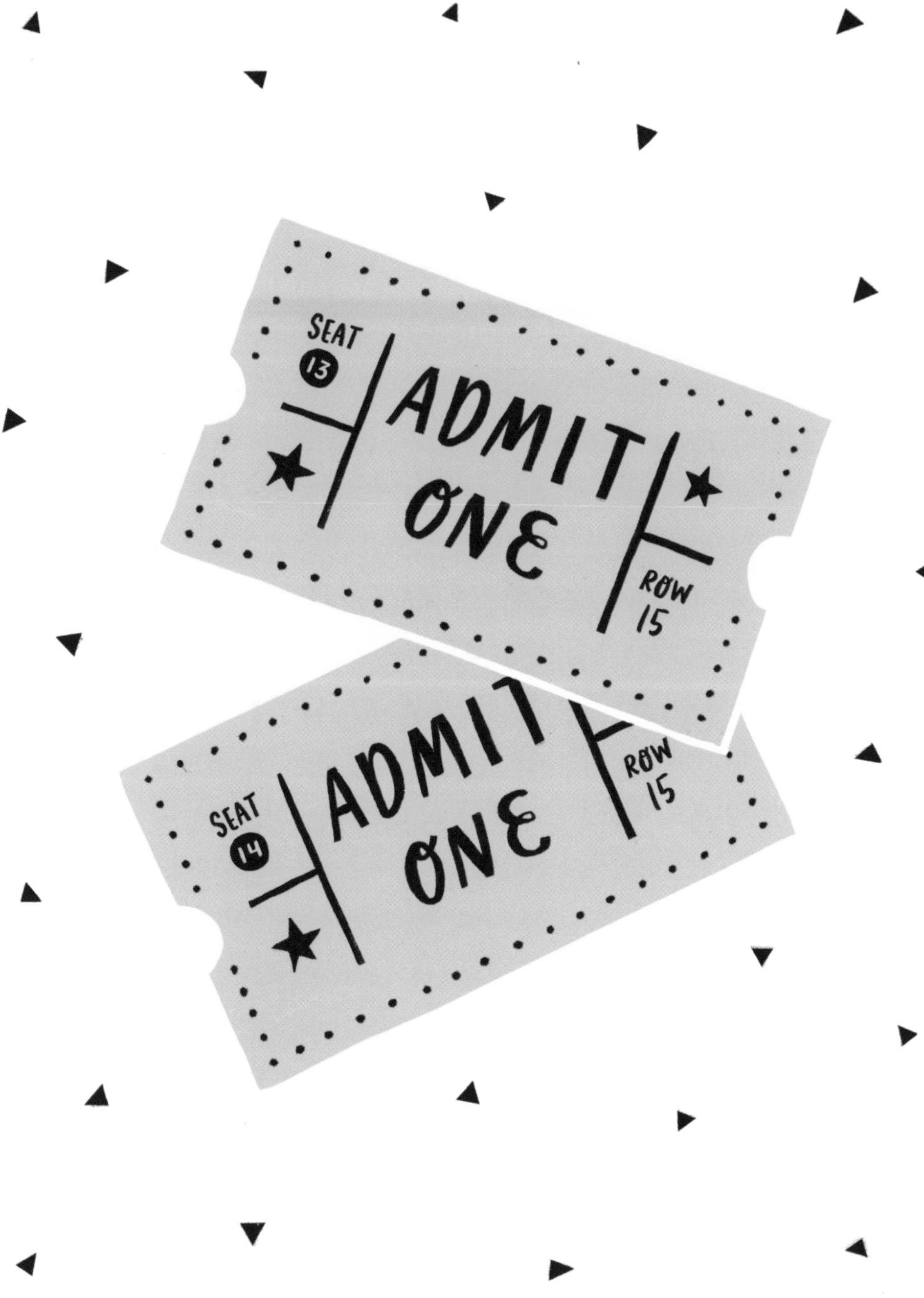
SEAT
13
ADMIT
ONE
ROW
15
SEAT
14
ADMIT
ONE
ROW
15

REMEMBERING GOOD TIMES *with you* IS EASY

...because they
actually happen
all the time.

YOU SEE THE HUMAN IN EVER

YBODY.

(Sometimes even when they AREN'T human.)

You always
think of others
before you think
of yourself.

LIKE HOW you NOTICE special THINGS AND POINT THEM OUT so no one else MISSES THEM.

YOU MAKE A LASTING *impression*

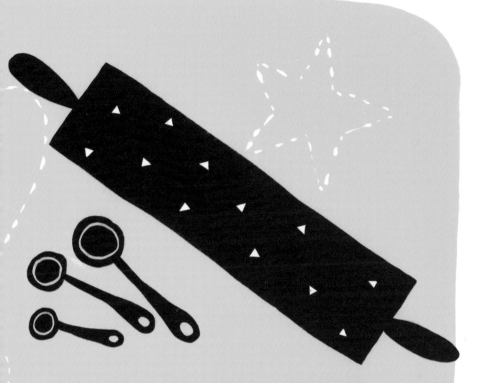

ON EVERYONE
WHO MEETS YOU.
(In a good way.)

CLOTHES

OFFICE
SUPPLIES

BLANKETS

BOOKS

DISHES

Heavy things
somehow feel
lighter with
you around.

YET YOU'RE STILL STRONG enough to HANDLE THE HEAVY THINGS.

Even colors are
a little bit
brighter with you.
(Thanks for that.)

HTY
at having
TALENTS.

A message FROM YOU IS LIKE GETTING a present

...and your
presents are always
thoughtful
and sincere.

You know when
to say something
and when to say
nothing at all.

IT'S EASY TO BE
honest
WITH YOU
BECAUSE YOU'RE
HONEST TOO.
In the kindest way.

YOU KNOW
HOW TO BE
altogether

EXTRAO

RDINARY.

You simply inspire others to be better humans...

JUST BY BEING exactly WHO YOU ARE.

(THANKS FOR THAT.)

COMPENDIUM.
live inspired

With special thanks to the entire Compendium family.

WRITTEN BY: MIRIAM HATHAWAY

DESIGNED & ILLUSTRATED BY: EMILY CARLSON

EDITED BY: AMELIA RIEDLER AND CINDY WETTERLUND

Library of Congress Control Number: 2019934994
ISBN: 978-1-946873-78-1

1st printing. Printed in China with soy inks.